Where Does Lightning & Thunder Come from?

Weather for Kids

(Preschool & Big Children Guide)

Where do amazing thunderstorms and lightning come from? Which comes first- lightning or thunder?

Read on and find out about lightning and thunder. Learn where they come from and if they are dangerous.

Kids, the study of lightning
is called fulminology.

It is fun to watch flashes
of lightning in the skies.
However, you should
not go out into the open
because lightning is
very dangerous. It can
cause you harm.

Are you afraid of thunder and lightning? If your honest answer is a resounding "yes!" then, sadly, you are suffering from "astraphobia".

It has been known that
lightning happens during
thunderstorms. What do
you call that loud bang
when there is lightning?
It is thunder. It is the loud
crack or the low rumble
that we hear on Earth.
It is caused by the heat
of the flash of lightning.

We see lightning before we hear thunder because light travels faster than sound. Amazingly, the speed of light which is approximately 669,600,000 miles per hour is faster than the speed of sound. This is pretty fantastic!

According to the
observation of Aristotle,
a Greek philosopher,
the collision of clouds
causes thunder. But
we know more now.
The lightning splits the
air it passes through,
and the bang is the air
closing back together.

What is a thunderstorm?

This is an electric storm
which causes lightning.
Sometimes, thunderstorms
are characterized by
heavy rain. When a
thunderstorm happens,
we hear see lightning
and we hear thunder.

Thunderstorms usually
happen during summer
when the weather is hot
and humid. The worst
of it happens in tropical
countries where the air is
very hot and very humid.
Every thunderstorm
has lightning.

Why is lightning
dangerous?

Lightning is a powerful
blow of electricity.

When does lightning occur?

When the ice and water particles inside thunder clouds are bumping around each other, lightning is produced. An electric charge is created when ice and water or rain particles are bumping each other. As they collide in the atmosphere an unbalanced charge is created. Lightning strikes when the electric charge connects with the electrical charges on the ground.

In the electrical charge, the electrons or the negative charge are formed at the bottom of the cloud. On the other hand, the protons or the positive charge is formed at the top of the cloud.

The negative charge will look for something with a positive charge on the ground in order to connect. Since opposites attract, the powerful burst of electricity happens. The lightning may strike at trees, a tall building or even a person. Lightning is one of the causes of the death of people. It is believed that every year, many people are struck by lightning.

We should hide at
home when lightning
strikes because it hits
tall objects on Earth.
Thunderstorms happen
anytime. They most occur
in the afternoon and
evening. More than 1,800
thunderstorms happen
on Earth every day.

Where does lightning occur?

Lightning may take place inside the thunderclouds, between clouds, and most especially from clouds to the ground.

Did you know that bolts of lightning are striking anywhere on Earth every second? Yes, lightning is actually striking the ground now! It is fatal because lightning carries a huge number of volts of electricity. Its average temperature is almost 20,000 °C. It is indeed very dangerous. More often, lightning seeks out its way on land than in the ocean.

Very tall and dense cumulonimbus clouds produce lightning. At other times, lightning is caused by volcanic eruptions, tornadoes, forest fires, and snow storms.

Kids, never go outside
during a thunderstorm. If
you happen to be
outside during a
thunderstorm, don't
go under a tree.

Visit
BABY PROFESSOR
EDUCATION KIDS
www.BabyProfessorBooks.com
to download Free Baby Professor eBooks
and view our catalog of new and exciting
Children's Books